BEGINNER'S GUIDE TO CORPORATE INSOLVENCY

COPYRIGHT

First published in Great Britain in 2021 under license to Jestina Media Limited
Registered office 78 York Street, London W1H 1DP

Publisher: Jestina Media Limited

ISBN: 978-1-8382617-1-9
Author: Peter Murray

Writer: Orantes Moore
orantesmoore@gmail.com

Editor: Akosua Annobil
aannobil@gmail.com

Creatives: Lasoke Creative Solutions

Layout and Print: CPUK Print Publishing
www.cp-uk.co.uk

CONTENTS

PROLOGUE

This book was written in 2020 in the midst of the Covid-19 pandemic. The UK government responded to this exceptional crisis by drafting radical new legislation to provide a lifeline for struggling businesses. The Corporate Insolvency and Governance Act was hurriedly enacted in June 2020 and introduced temporary and permanent changes to the laws relating to companies and insolvency. Included in these sweeping amendments were a raft of debtor-friendly measures designed to curb company collapses and stabilise the UK's flagging economy.

Consequently, the Act significantly increased the options available to a company director or business owner seeking to rescue and/or restructure a profitable but insolvent company. For example, the Corporate Insolvency and Governance Act:

- Introduced a moratorium facility that provides companies with protection from creditors and a two-month window to develop a rescue plan
- Provided some company directors with immunity from prosecution for wrongful trading between 1 March 2020 and 30 September 2020
- Temporarily restricted the filing of statutory demands on Covid-19-related debts (effective until 31 December 2020 at the time of writing)
- Temporarily restricted the issuing of winding-up petitions on Covid-19-related debts (effective until 31 December 2020 at the time of writing)

• The temporary suspension of debt enforcement measures hinders creditors from collecting due payments while offering companies and their directors/ owners an extraordinary amount of protection, so they have time to plan and restructure to succeed with a winding-up petition, the petitioner must prove the company remains insolvent and was doomed to fail irrespective of Covid-19 (which is only practical for debts incurred in 2019 and some exceptional circumstances thereafter).

In accordance with the Act's temporary measures, a creditor's only debt enforcement remedies are through the county court via either a bailiff or a third-party debt order. In response, some debtors defend the claim, and keep the action going for 12 to 18 months to prolong simply to prolong court proceedings. Since the introduction of the Act, it is perfectly acceptable and credible for a debtor to say:

'We'd planned to pay you a few months ago from the proceeds of a payment that was due to be made by a customer. But Covid-19 affected their business and they've been unable to pay, which is why I'm currently unable to pay you.'

Another controversial provision of the Corporate Insolvency and Governance Act temporarily suspends the use of termination clauses for many medium- and large-sized companies. This component prevents their suppliers/creditors from using the terms and conditions in their contracts to stop the supply of 'essential' goods and services to a company in a statutory insolvency procedure. However, affected suppliers/creditors have a valid defence to help avoid the suspension if they are able to respond by saying:

'Because of Covid-19, I don't have the resources to purchase the materials I need to supply you as normal.'

Arguably, some of the measures in the Corporate Insolvency and Governance Act are too debtor-friendly, as they can easily be abused by an unscrupulous or rogue director who deliberately takes in as many supplies as possible knowing it's unlikely all of the company's creditors will be paid everything they're owed.

I wrote this book after searching online and discovering little credible information to assist directors of insolvent companies, and other debtors seeking representation or to represent themselves in procedures such as:

- Administration
- Bankruptcy
- Company voluntary arrangement (CVA)
- Creditors' voluntary liquidation (CVL)
- Individual voluntary arrangement (IVA)

Aside from charities such as the Citizen's Advice Bureau (which are helpful but ill-equipped and offer limited knowledge), there is effectively nowhere debtors and defendants involved in insolvency proceedings and litigation can go for guidance and support. Therefore, I hope this helps.

DEBTOR REPRESENTATION

What is Debtor Representation?

Debtor Representation is an informal procedure conducted on a client's behalf and under their instructions. Creditors are approached in an attempt to negotiate deals to delay or reduce the amount the debtor owes. This is done without having to enter a formal insolvency process such as a voluntary arrangement (VA).

Do You Need Debtor Representation?

You probably need debtor representation if you are under duress from creditors. These include harassing:

- Telephone calls
- Emails
- Letters
- Formal demands
- Threats of bailiff or court action

And undue pressure from:

- HM Revenue & Customs (HMRC)
- Banks
- Suppliers
- Other creditors

Worse still, threats with a:

- Winding-up petition
- Bankruptcy petition

DEFENDING COUNTY COURT CLAIMS AND CCJS

What is a County Court Money Claim?

According to Part 7 of the Ministry of Justice's Civil Procedure Rules, any person or business can apply to a county court to demand payment of an unpaid debt.

Before applying for a county court money claim, a claimant should first serve the debtor with a pre-action letter. This is a formal notice explaining the circumstances surrounding the debt and requesting payment within 14 days. The claimant can make a county court money claim if the defendant (debtor) fails to pay or reach an agreement to pay.

After the claimant has commenced proceedings, the court will issue a county court notice to be served on the debtor who has 14 days to acknowledge receipt. At this stage, the defendant has three choices:

1) Pay the debt in full.
2) Pay what they believe they owe.
3) Ask for an additional 14 days to defend the claim.

When a defendant fails to respond in time, they are deemed to have accepted the debt. This could lead the claimant to apply to the county court for a default judgment

ACKNOWLEDGEMENT OF SERVICE AND DEFAULT JUDGMENT

To defend the claim, you must file an 'acknowledgement of service' form. Upon receipt, the court will notify the claimant and prepare to process the claim. If no defence is filed, the claimant can complete and file a 'request for judgment' form for the court to order a judgment in default. Still, judgments in default can be set aside because the court has only heard from one party.

Mediation

Before scheduling hearing dates, the court will write to both parties and suggest settling the dispute through mediation. They will recommend attending a mediation centre and sharing the costs for hiring a mediator at a rate of around £1,500 a day.

Alternatively, each party is free to:

- Hire their own solicitors and barristers
- Go through the process unrepresented to keep costs down

If a settlement is reached, it is always good to draw up either a consent order or a Tomlin order to document details of the agreement, which becomes legally binding once the order has been received and sealed by the court. If mediation fails or breaks down, the parties return to court.

It is worth considering that if a claimant refuses to enter mediation, continues to prosecute the claim and wins, the defendant can argue they should not be held liable for the claimant's costs as both parties' expenses would have reduced if they had entered mediation. In such circumstances, the court may:

- Agree and recommend the defendant pay none or 50% of the costs
- Disagree and order the defendant to pay full costs

Small Claims

For small claims of less than £10,000, neither party is entitled to recover their costs. As a result, it is sometimes better for debtors to represent themselves as neither party will recoup their legal expenses.

For example, if a law firm charges £500 to issue a claim for a £9,000 debt, which is later defended, they may request further payment of £3,000 to £4,000 to litigate the claim through to trial. Even if the lawyers are successful, the claimant will still be out of pocket, having spent £3,000 to £4,000 recovering £9,000.

In contrast, debtors who represent themselves would be operating from a position of strength in negotiations because they have no litigation costs.

Frustrating the Court Process

Generally, it takes months for a claim to go to trial and as a result it is very easy for a debtor to hinder or stall the process by:

- Continuously filing interim court applications
- Constantly making court applications in an effort to outspend the claimant
- Another strategy employed by litigants is to be unavailable for court dates.

Costs

Debtors love county courts because even the most flimsy defence can buy them an additional six months for a debt they had originally agreed to pay within 30 days. As a result, it is normal for claimants to spend £10,000 to £15,000 trying to recover a £30,000 debt. Even if the claimant wins the case, by the end of the trial the debtor would have had their £30,000 for 12 to 18 months. Moreover, it has become conventional that when the claimant tries to collect payment, they discover the debtor company has collapsed and reconstituted elsewhere.

Tips for Defendants

A shrewd debtor, who has no intention of paying, could create a dispute to prevent a claimant from issuing a winding-up petition on the debtor company. But a debtor with a weak defence should consider settling or quickly coming to some kind of arrangement.

In truth, the claimant will probably be happy to take 50% of the debt immediately, rather than waiting six to 12 months and paying legal fees for a trial that may not result in a favourable outcome. A debtor is under no pressure because time is on their side, so why not approach the claimant with a view to settling?

A savvy debtor with a weak defence who wants to maximise their leverage should consider utilising Part 36 of the Civil Procedure Rules, which encourages parties to settle disputes without going to trial. Under Part 36, every settlement offer is made on a 'without prejudice save as to costs' basis, so:

- Any deals and negotiations are kept secret until after the court has reached a judgment
- If one party rejects an offer and the claim goes to trial, they will probably be made to pay costs for both sides if the case goes against them

For example, under Part 36, a debtor who owes £30,000 may say: *'Rather than going to trial and both of us spending thousands of pounds in litigation fees, I'll pay you £15,000 to settle the claim now.'*

If the court rules the debtor is only liable for £15,000, and they subsequently reveal the claimant rejected a proposed settlement, the court, at the debtor's request, may order the claimant to pay their legal fees because the claim could have been settled earlier.

Part 36 offers are useful for debtors with a weak defence who want to settle quickly. Although some bloody-minded claimants will fight for the principle until the bitter end, few have the patience for a long battle and will take what they can get. Also, if you are defending a claim against a person or business who owes you money, you may consider counterclaiming.

For example, a landlord who has been served a county court claim for £20,000 from an electrician might say:

'Even though I owe you £20,000, the work you did was substandard so I had to get another electrician to fix your repairs and the original problem. They charged £25,000, which I'm claiming against you. Let's forget about the £5,000 difference and call it quits. But if you continue with your claim for £20,000, I'll continue with mine for £25,000.'

HOW TO RESPOND TO A STATUTORY DEMAND

Never ignore a statutory demand. Failure to respond could result in the winding up of a limited company or bankruptcy for an individual. A statutory demand (stat demand or stat d) is a formal document requesting payment of an outstanding debt within 21 days. Anyone can make a statutory demand for a debt that's less than six years old.

It may take some time to reach an agreement with a creditor. This will depend on how the debtor wishes to proceed and their company's (or personal) circumstance. Additionally, they may have to apply to the court to have the statutory demand set aside or an uncooperative creditor restrained.

The debtor has three main remedies for dealing with a statutory demand. But these actions must be taken early:

1) Make arrangements to pay all or part of the debt.
2) Dispute the debt either partially or entirely.
3) Pay the debt within 18 days.

Disputed Debts

There are several ways to respond to a disputed statutory demand. First, you can reply in writing, within 21 days, by setting out in detail the grounds for the dispute. If you follow up with an invitation to withdraw the statutory demand, the creditor would be wise to oblige.

Also, you can apply to the court to have the statutory demand set aside and dismissed if the debt is disputed or more than six years old. But this must be done within 18 days of receiving the statutory demand.

Court Injunctions

In the instance of a limited company debtor, you can apply for injunctive relief if a creditor refuses to withdraw the statutory demand after they have been notified of a dispute. If the court injunction is granted, they will probably have to pay your legal expenses, which could cost between £5,000 and £15,000 or more if the injunction is unsuccessfully resisted.

The legal grounds for defending a statutory demand can be technical. As a result, it's crucial to seek advice from an independent insolvency specialist on how best to proceed.

Counterclaim

The counterclaim is another effective strategy that can be used to challenge a statutory demand. You can neutralise a creditor and gain considerable leverage if your claim for direct, indirect or consequential loss is worth more than their claimed debt.

DEFENDING A BANKRUPTCY PETITION

There used to be a stigma associated with bankruptcy. However, the Enterprise Act 2002 introduced a rescue culture to British business that softened bankruptcy regulations and encouraged entrepreneurialism.

Benefits of Bankruptcy

Prior to the introduction of the Enterprise Act, discharges took three years and remained on file for 11 years. Now, bankrupts are discharged after 12 months and the process is removed from your credit report after six years.

In many instances, bankruptcy is a viable option especially if you get to keep your home and income. The procedure will affect your credit rating, but unless you have assets or surplus income very little changes and life will resume as usual after the bankrupt is discharged.

What is a Trustee?

In bankruptcy, the function of a trustee (insolvency practitioner) is comparable to that of an administrator or liquidator in the insolvency of a limited company. Irrespective of the procedure, the insolvency practitioner's main task is to realise assets to pay creditors. Aside from the tools of your trade, absolutely everything is up for grabs.

A trustee is a 'supervisor' in Company Voluntary Arrangements (CVAs) and Individual Voluntary Arrangements (IVAs).

Debtor's Bankruptcy Petition

If you cannot pay your debts, you may apply to a court to be declared bankrupt. You must provide a statement of affairs, which details the debts and explains that you have no means to pay. The bankruptcy application costs £680. The application and a list of the debtor's assets and liabilities should be sent to an adjudicator at the government's Insolvency Service.

The adjudicator will assess the information and decide if you should be made bankrupt. Although creditors may object, they rarely do. Any attempt to hide assets or frustrate the bankruptcy could lead to an indefinite suspension. In most cases, the process is a relatively harmless one from which you will be automatically discharged exactly one year after the bankruptcy order was first made.

You will still have to pay court fines, student loans and child maintenance. But if you have no surplus income after you are discharged, most of your debts will die and creditors will not be able to chase you.

Official Receiver Examination

After you have been declared bankrupt, you will be summoned for an interview with the official receiver. They are court-appointed officials from the Insolvency Service. They will ask you to fill out a questionnaire with information about your:

- Assets
- Liabilities
- Income

- Employment
- Bank account(s)
- Life insurance

If you have valuable assets, the official receiver will appoint an insolvency practitioner to act as trustee. The insolvency practitioner will sell your assets to pay the creditors.

How to Avoid Being Made Bankrupt

A company director or business owner can avoid a creditors' bankruptcy petition simply by disputing the debt. Although some courts may not permit a creditor to dispute the claim on the grounds the challenge should have been raised in the 21-day period after the statutory demand was served, other courts will be reluctant to declare a person bankrupt over a disputed debt.

An individual can circumvent a bankruptcy petition by proposing to enter an Individual Voluntary Agreement (IVA). If you are employed or have a steady income, an IVA may be a better option than bankruptcy because the process allows debtors up to five years to repay creditors.

IPOs and IPAs

If your trustee believes you have surplus revenue, they can ask the court to make you pay up to 36 monthly payments into the bankruptcy estate via an income payments order (IPO). Alternatively, you can make these payments voluntarily through an income payment agreement (IPA). The fee for each is approximately £150 and will be taken from your first payment.

After-Acquired Assets

Monies and after-acquired assets, such as a lottery win or court case payout obtained during the bankruptcy period, are usually placed into the bankruptcy estate where the proceeds will be used to pay creditors.

Hiding Assets

If the official receiver suspects a bankrupt is hiding money or assets, they will probably appoint a trustee to dig around to see if anything can be recovered.The trustee may conduct investigations in territories outside the jurisdiction of UK courts and if successful, seize anything of value they find.

Antecedent Transactions

It is strictly forbidden for a bankrupt to (before being made bankrupt):

- Sell assets at undervalue
- Acquire an excessive amount of credit
- Make preferential payments to creditors
- Deliberately dissipate assets to deprive creditors
- Place assets beyond the reach of creditors

The trustee may seek the court's permission to cancel and set aside any antecedent transactions (dealings that were harmful to the interest of creditors) that took place in the months prior to the bankruptcy.

Keeping Your Home in Bankruptcy

Arguably the biggest stigma associated with bankruptcy is the fear of losing the family home. But this can be avoided in some cases. Even if a trustee really wants to take the property, the courts will not allow this during the first 12 months.

However, after one year creditors' interests prevail, so the trustee can take steps towards seizing and selling your home if there is significant equity in the property. But they must first instruct lawyers to draft an order and make an application to a court. Litigation costs on both sides will escalate if the bankrupt resists and contests. Subsequently, the trustee will be left with a sizeable legal bill, even if they do eventually get the property.

If one owner becomes bankrupt but the couple want to keep the house, the other party must buy back the 50% share now controlled by the trustee. Even if they refuse to buy the share, the trustee can force the sale of the property after 12 months.

It is unlikely a trustee will be concerned about a property with less than £10,000 in equity because after paying for the charges and solicitor's fees, they know they will be lucky to end up with £3,000. What is more likely is the trustee may say:

'Arrange for me to receive a third-party payment of £6,000 and I'll disclaim my interest in your property.'

If a bankrupt really wants to keep their home and there is significant equity in the property, they can arrange for a third-party payment to the trustee for a corresponding amount. For example, if a trustee who wants your home says: *'I think there's £50,000 equity in the property,'* your response should be to get the house valued, whereby your beneficial share is worth £30,000.

Even if the trustee successfully contests the appraisal, it will take them at least 12 to 18 months to collect any money, and after paying all expenses they would probably only receive £25,000. Subsequently, you could offer the trustee a cash sum of £24,000 (payable in 12 monthly instalments of £2,000) to disclaim their interest in the property and they would probably take it.

HMRC TIME TO PAY (TTP) ARRANGEMENT

Are you considering a Time to Pay (TTP) arrangement because either you or your business is struggling with Her Majesty's Revenue & Customs (HMRC) debts? If you are still reading, you probably have an unresolved problem with HMRC or owe them money. You may have received a:

- Warning letter
- Statutory demand
- Bankruptcy petition
- Winding-up petition

Time to Pay is an informal agreement that provides debtors with an opportunity to demonstrate they take their HMRC debt seriously. To qualify, debtors must agree to pay all of their current liabilities on time. Additionally, you must repay any historic debts over six to 12 months, depending on the agreement terms. The process is pretty much the same whether you are approaching HMRC as an individual or a company.

Benefits of TTP

It is helpful if you can explain how in your particular circumstance Time to Pay is a better alternative than statutory insolvency procedures. For example, a TTP arrangement is far more appealing than a Company Voluntary Arrangement

(CVA) or an Individual Voluntary Arrangement (IVA), which pay out less money and take up to five years to conclude. In summary, a debtor's conversation with HMRC should go something like this:

'I concede that my company owes £100,000. If you agree to a TTP arrangement, we'll clear these tax debts by paying £10,000 a month over 10 months. But if you reject our proposition, I'll probably be forced into either an IVA or a CVA, and under those circumstances it's likely that you'll only receive £1,000-a-month for 60 months.'

Few debtors are aware of the leverage they have because TTP is the far more attractive option. However, it's probably best to remain humble because if you are too arrogant HMRC will simply wind up your company or present you with a bankruptcy petition if you are an individual.

INDIVIDUAL VOLUNTARY ARRANGEMENT (IVA)

What is an IVA?

An Individual Voluntary Arrangement (IVA) is a legally binding and court-approved agreement a person makes with their creditors to pay all or part of their debts. The procedures for IVAs and Company Voluntary Arrangements (CVAs) are almost identical. However, a protocol exists that simplifies the process for an IVA comprising consumer-based debts.

When most of the debt has been acquired through regulated credit agreements, such as bank loans and credit cards, creditors are automatically compliant and must have a very good reason to reject the IVA.

Pros and Cons

It is important to ensure that the terms of the Individual Voluntary Arrangement are in your best interest and right for you. Each proposal is different and in many instances the monthly contributions could be significantly lower than what creditors propose.

Many IVAs fail to survive the duration and as a consequence bankruptcy becomes inevitable. To avoid this happening to you, never enter an IVA without first seeking professional, independent advice to guide you through the proposal stage.

Applying for an IVA

To apply for an Individual Voluntary Arrangement, you must approach an insolvency practitioner to facilitate the agreement. Insolvency practitioners are known as 'nominees' before the proposal is agreed and 'supervisors' afterwards.

Your insolvency practitioner will help you calculate how much and how frequently you can afford to pay. Part of their job is to collect money from you before distributing those funds equally among your creditors. If you're unable to pay off all of your debts, the rest will be written off as an act of 'debt forgiveness'. The Individual Voluntary Arrangement will commence after creditors representing at least 75% of the total debt value agree to the proposal.

If you fail to keep up with your repayments, the supervisor will terminate the agreement and you could be made bankrupt. You should seriously consider whether an IVA or an alternative such as bankruptcy is the best option for you.

Length of an IVA

The maximum term for an Individual Voluntary Arrangement is usually five years. However, the agreement could be completed sooner if your financial circumstances improve and you are able to increase the amount paid out to creditors. Someone who pays creditors 40% of what is owed at the start of the IVA may be able to pay 70% after receiving a pay rise or if a dependent gains full-time employment.

Equity in Your House

If you enter an Individual Voluntary Arrangement and have a property with equity that increases in value, creditors can try and force you to release the equity for their benefit when the agreement ends.

For example, before voting to approve your IVA a savvy creditor who anticipates the equity in your property will grow from £20,000 to £50,000 throughout the duration of the agreement, might say:

'We'll approve your Individual Voluntary Arrangement. But we'd like to make some modifications to the proposal, including a provision stating that at the end of the term you'll either pay creditors £30,000 or sell the property.'

An insolvency practitioner may not advise you of this situation in the hope they eventually gain control of the property for themselves. Secretly, they'll anticipate that you continue growing the equity by paying the mortgage, but fail the IVA just before the agreement ends. In these circumstances, a supervisor can:

- Petition for you to be made bankrupt
- Become the trustee of your bankruptcy
- Gain access to the equity in your house

COMPANY VOLUNTARY ARRANGEMENT (CVA)

What is a CVA?

A Company Voluntary Arrangement (CVA) is a formal contract between an insolvent company and its creditors. They allow companies to continue trading while repaying creditors, usually over a period of three to five years.

In many instances, a company seeking a CVA is experiencing a slump in sales following a successful period of trading. Sometimes,one or two bad trades can render a company insolvent and cause historic debt to build while directors try to resolve the problem. But in most cases, an otherwise good and profitable business has become insolvent and can no longer trade because of:

- Bad business decisions
- Lost customers
- Too much debt
- A combination of all three

Benefits of a Company Voluntary Arrangement

Company Voluntary Arrangements give company directors an opportunity to approach creditors and say:

'We have a good business moving forward. But we've collected some historic debt that we can't service. A proposal is being put together for us to enter an arrangement that allows the company to continue trading while repaying a

percentage of what we owe you over the next five years.'

For example, the director(s) of a company with £1m of debt may agree to pay 50% with 60 successive monthly instalments of £8,333.34 and ask creditors to write off the remaining £500,000 as an act of 'debt forgiveness'.

The director(s) of an insolvent company are prohibited from trading and can be held personally liable for any new debts the business acquires. Subsequently, in most instances creditors are likely to accept the proposal as the alternative will result in the company being placed into liquidation.

How Does a Company Enter a CVA?

The process begins when a company director(s) seeks out and hires an insolvency practitioner, known as a 'nominee', to put together a Company Voluntary Arrangement proposal. Nominees usually take four to six weeks to prepare the proposal and charge between £8,000 and £10,000. The proposal normally includes:

- Financial data
- A synopsis of the company's trading history
- Information about the directors, creditors, shareholders and employees
- Three- to five-year restructuring projections explaining how the business will become profitable and pay monthly into the CVA

Additionally, the proposal sets out the fees charged by the nominee, who becomes a 'supervisor' after the terms have been ratified. Supervisors collect monthly installments from the company totaling £30,000 to £40,000, which they distribute to creditors once or twice a year.

The director(s) sign off the proposal in the form of a sworn affidavit and a creditors' meeting is convened. In the affidavit, the nominee will state:

'...the proposal is fit, fair and feasible, and has a good chance of success.'

If the company falls into more than two months' arrears on their contributions to creditors, the CVA will be deemed to have failed and the supervisor will be obliged to wind the company up. Ironically, although insolvency practitioners rarely tell creditors the proposal will fail, around 50% of companies that enter CVAs fall into liquidation within five years, which suggests that a worrying number of insolvency practitioners make erroneous assessments.

How is a CVA Proposal Approved?

A group of creditors who are owed at least 75% of the debt must vote in favour of the proposal for a CVA to be approved. They can do this via email, virtual meetings or some other correspondence.

Connected Creditors

After friends and relatives of the director(s) who have lent money to the company (connected creditors) are removed from the equation, 50% of the remaining creditors must be in favour for the proposal to be successful.

Dos and Don'ts

Your company can continue to trade and sell goods but is forbidden from paying long-standing debts during the two months it takes the nominee to prepare the proposal. Consequently, surplus cash reserves build up which enable corrupt directors to say to friendly creditors:

'According to the proposal, the company has agreed to pay 35% of all debts. But if you vote to get the CVA approved, I'll secretly pay your debt in full.'

It is a sad truth, but some company directors approach insolvency procedures as mechanisms to grow their business. As a result, Company Voluntary Arrangements have become popular, especially as they are less expensive than alternatives such as a pre-pack administration. Moreover, the insolvency practitioner in a pre-pack must investigate the director's conduct. In contrast, a director applying for a CVA faces little scrutiny because sufficient debt has been written off to make the company solvent. Additionally, creditors have ratified the proposal and agreed to continue trading.

Some devious company directors plan their Company Voluntary Arrangement up to one year in advance. For example, they may purchase £1m of additional stock in the months leading up to the CVA process and then offer to repay creditors £500,000 in the CVA proposal. Essentially, they pay £500,000 for goods worth £1m, and have 60 months to pay the debt without incurring any interest. It is the deal of the century.

It is unlikely the director could secure a loan with such generous terms from their bank; so, creditors effectively become the company's de-facto banker, providing an interest-free loan payable over five years with a 65% discount. As mentioned, there is an approximately 50% chance the CVA will fail, so most creditors never receive the money they have been promised. Additionally, the CVA will probably make the company super-competitive because it's been able to acquire goods for 65% less than any of its competitors and can therefore sell them much cheaper than anyone else.

Director(s) will naturally seek out an insolvency practitioner they feel comfortable with, even though insolvency practitioners are prohibited from providing independent advice, and should act to protect creditors' interests. Subsequently, director(s) contemplating a CVA should consider the terms of the agreement. It is important to ensure they are beneficial and appropriate for the situation.

PLACING YOUR COMPANY INTO ADMINISTRATION

What is Administration?

Administration is a procedure that functions as a rescue mechanism for asset-rich but insolvent companies, in accordance with Schedule B1 of the Insolvency Act 1986. Administration is usually a precursor or alternative to liquidation. The procedure allows a business to be:

- Rescued as a going concern
- Sold as whole
- Offloaded in parts to realise cash for creditors

How Does Administration Differ From Liquidation?

Liquidation is the end of the road, similar to switching off a company's life support machine. In contrast, entering administration is like being connected to a life support machine. The company may:

- Expire
- Be sold as a going concern
- Continue to exist through either a pre-pack administration or a Company Voluntary Arrangement (CVA)

Generally, administrations are expensive, quickly devouring a company's cash and leaving very little, if anything, for creditors. Administration normally results in a company's swift demise, especially if the business cannot be sold immediately as a going concern. Although the procedure provides protection from creditors who are threatening legal action, the director(s) must concede full control of the company's management and future to the administrator.

Administration Orders

Following an application to court for an administration order, there are three ways a company can be placed into administration:

- In court
- Out of court
- If a charge holder (creditor) invites an insolvency practitioner (administrator) to act as interim chief executive with custodial responsibility for the company's obligations and assets

Director(s) of a company they deem insolvent can activate an out-of-court administration. This involves:

- Filing an application to the court
- Making and signing an affidavit or witness statement
- Calling in an insolvency practitioner to confirm the company's insolvency

Court Administration

To activate a court administration, directors or creditors can present evidence of the company's insolvency. Creditors and other third parties can object when the application is heard by a court judge. Creditors are free to contact the administrator and arrange to purchase the business in part or as a whole. They must put in tenders and the administrator is likely to sell the business to the highest bidder. Alternatively, a director can cleanse the business by arranging to purchase some or all of its assets in a pre-pack.

Pre-pack Administrations

Entrepreneurial business owners who have overtraded often use preppacks to:

- Buy back the core assets of the business
- Start trading again under a new company name

However, there are potential conflict-of-interest issues associated with this type of procedure as the administrator's employment depends largely on whether their valuation of the business is agreeable to the director(s) (who is both seller and buyer). So, if the director(s) is unhappy with the appraisal, they are unlikely to hire the administrator to coordinate the pre-pack.

For example, an unscrupulous director whose company owes creditors £300,000 may consider a pre-pack a viable option and try to undervalue the business. The director will know the main components (brand, business model, intellectual property, customer database, stock, market share, goodwill etc) value £250,000. But when an insolvency practitioner is called in, the director can mislead them by claiming the business is only worth £50,000 to £100,000. Still, the insolvency practitioner must obtain professional appraisals from two independent sources that are likely to reveal the true value.

Usually in such cases, when the insolvency practitioner sends their valuation report, the director(s) will refuse to acknowledge its findings and start searching for someone else. If the insolvency practitioner wants the job, they're likely to compromise by finding a new appraiser to value the business at around £120,000, and persuade the director(s) to agree to the revised evaluation. This may require additional time, and a further valuation if the director is inflexible.

Once a price is agreed upon, the insolvency practitioner will put the business out for tender and create a detailed prospectus containing relevant information about the business, which prospective buyers receive after signing a nondisclosure agreement. Sometimes, if the insolvency practitioner has already decided to sell the business to the director, they may create an unattractive prospectus to encourage other potential buyers to enter low bids.

Depending on the insolvency practitioner's trustworthiness, they will either:

1) Facilitate the sale to the director, or

2) Follow protocol by advertising the tender to a database of prospective buyers who will put in sealed bids before a specified deadline.

If no one else bids, the insolvency practitioner will sell the business to the director(s). They are supposed to sell to the highest bidder, but the company has not yet officially entered administration so the director(s) can say to the insolvency practitioner:

'If you don't sell the business to me, you're not getting the job.'

Out-of-Court Administration

First, a Sale and Purchase Agreement (SPA) between the director(s) and administrator will be drawn up. Secondly, the director(s) or a representative will go to court. They should bring the agreement and the application for an out-of-court appointment, which the court typically rubber stamps. Usually, the director(s) buys back the company's assets on the same day the business goes into administration. The premises and staff usually stay the same, it is just the company name that changes.

Advice for Directors

Legally, administrators must report the conduct of the director(s) to the Secretary of State for Business, Energy and Industrial Strategy. Their report will explain the reason for the company's failure. The director(s) could be held personally liable if the report is damaging and includes wrongdoing or misconduct. In addition to administration, there are alternative insolvency procedures that may be favourable depending on your particular circumstance.

Directors hold all the cards in a pre-pack because they know how much they are willing to pay for the business and are free to appoint an insolvency practitioner of their choice to facilitate the sale. Furthermore, after a price has been agreed, the director can suggest paying in instalments, which means they effectively end up paying nothing for the business.

For example, if a director offers to pay the administrator 12 monthly instalments of £10,000 for a business valued at £120,000, they will not be spending from their own pocket because that money is coming out of the insolvent business. The director(s) knows that after the pre-pack, the assets will help to generate the income necessary to make the monthly payments and the creditors will be the only thing they lose from the original business.

But any sensible insolvency practitioner who agreed to those payment terms would want some form of security from the director(s), such as a personal guarantee. The insolvency practitioner and creditors are effectively lending the director(s) cash to buy back the business, but whereas creditors get shafted, the insolvency practitioner gets paid.

PLACING YOUR COMPANY INTO CREDITORS' VOLUNTARY LIQUIDATION (CVL)

Meeting of Shareholders

Although the process is called a creditors' voluntary liquidation (CVL), the directors decide whether the company is able to meet its obligations and commitments. If the director(s) decide the company is insolvent, they must:

- Call a meeting of shareholders
- Convince 75% of shareholders to wind up the company
- Nominate an insolvency practitioner to coordinate the liquidation

Insolvency practitioners act as liquidators on behalf of the court and have far-reaching statutory duties. However, strictly speaking they do not operate as officers of the court in a CVL.

Role of the Liquidator

The liquidator will examine and investigate:

- The company director(s)
- The company's affairs
- Reasons why the company has failed
- All the company's contracts, which terminate on the date of liquidation

Liquidators will analyse all your company's transactions to establish if they were made in the interest of the creditors. Following their investigations, the liquidator is legally obliged to file a confidential report on the director's conduct (commonly known as a D-Report) to the Insolvency Service.

The report will contain explanations for the company's failure, including any serious misconduct on your part, and offer insight into:

- How the company started
- What it does
- How it became insolvent

Before commencement of the liquidation, the director(s) (assisted by the liquidator) must prepare a statement of affairs for the company, which is signed off by the director(s) and made available to creditors prior to the liquidation date.

The statement of affairs includes:

- A summarised version of management accounts from the last accounting period up to the present date
- A statement of affairs comprising statutory data
- Consolidated summarised accounts for the previous three years
- Information about any legal proceedings
- The company's trading history
- Reason(s) for its failure
- A schedule describing the company's assets
- An estimate of their realised value
- A list detailing each creditor's name and address and how much they are owed

A liquidator who suspects that transactions were made to the detriment of creditors may take various courses of action, including asking the director(s) to remedy the loss by paying into the liquidation estate.

Dos and Don'ts

If your company has received a court winding up order and become the subject of compulsory liquidation proceedings, you will need to consider seriously your general conduct as a director. Any actions you have taken or failed to take that led to your company's demise will require due consideration. This period of reflection will need to cover the three most recent years of your directorship.

A director must act and behave very differently when their company is insolvent. You should take steps to protect and maximise the company's assets and reduce its liabilities in the interest of all creditors without favour or preference.

Even if you are not recorded as a director at Companies House, you may still be held as a shadow director, especially if your decisions and actions influenced the promotion or management of the company and contributed to its demise. Shadow directors are treated as appointed directors, so they can be held personally liable.

If you are asked but fail to make a contribution into the liquidation estate, the liquidator or another party may bring a claim for misfeasance against you. If these proceedings are successful, you could be:

- Ordered to make a financial restoration into the liquidation estate.
- Disqualified from being a company director for a period of two to 15 years.

Similarly, a director exposes suppliers and other creditors to unnecessary risk by trading with an insolvent company, and continuing to obtain credit they cannot pay for. Wrongful trading is a breach of a director's fiduciary duties and thus another misfeasance under section 214 of the Insolvency Act 1986.

You must be confident that your conduct was lawful because the liquidator has a legal duty to act in the interest of the company's creditors. Consequently, they cannot be relied upon to provide independent advice.

A director with a company facing liquidation should avoid:

- Contravening the Insolvency Act 1986 or the Companies Act 2006
- Being indebted to the company by way of an overdrawn director's loan account
- Making preferential payments

Many directors are caught borrowing money from the business and become one of the company's debtors when it falls into insolvency. Liquidators regard directors in this position as low-hanging fruit and will quickly target them for money.

Another major pitfall to avoid is making preferential payments to creditors as this contravenes section 239 of the Insolvency Act 1986. If a company is insolvent, all creditors must be treated equally so paying one while ignoring another is strictly forbidden.

For example, when a director uses their loan account to lend the company money they automatically become a creditor of the company. As a result, if the business becomes insolvent it is forbidden for that director to have the loan repaid before the business goes into liquidation. Unlike the company's other creditors, they would have known the business was failing and thus given themselves an unfair and preferential payment. And it is the same thing with other parties; there should be no preferential payments to any suppliers, partners, stakeholders or even family members.

Similarly, section 238 of the Insolvency Act prohibits the sale or transfer of company assets for less than their market value either prior to or during the winding-up process. Any transaction at undervalue deprives creditors of the monies they are owed and is considered a misfeasance.

There are various provisions of the Insolvency Act relating to a director's behaviour. They include sections 423 and 245, which respectively prohibit transactions that defraud creditors and the granting of charges when the company is insolvent or likely to become insolvent.

It is important to remember that creditors place a huge amount of trust in directors, and in most cases trade without any knowledge of the company's liabilities, bank balance or debts. Therefore, it is essential that a company director is seen to be operating in the interests of all, and not just some, creditors.

RESPONDING TO A WINDING-UP PETITION

What is a Winding-up Petition?

A winding-up petition is a court application, usually obtained by a disgruntled creditor to force an insolvent company into compulsory liquidation. Winding-up petitions can be issued against companies that fail to pay their debts on time.

Consequences

The serving of a winding-up petition should concern a company director because section 127 of the Insolvency Act 1986 is immediately triggered. Under section 127, directors are forbidden from taking several actions, including making payments from the company's bank account(s) without first obtaining the court's permission.

For example, a director would be unable to access the company's account(s) to pay for a customer's coffee during a business meeting. To regain control of the company and stop the winding-up process, the debtor/director must clear the debt before the court hearing. This shows the business is solvent and able to pay its debts when they are due.

Seven working days after the petition has been served, the petitioner/creditor can publicise the winding up in *The London Gazette* newspaper, which publishes statutory notices, and is the UK Government's primary journal of record. During those seven working days, the debtor/director can defend the company by going to court for either an injunction or a validation order.

If the winding-up petition is ignored and no validation order or injunction has been obtained, the petition may be advertised in the newspaper and the company's bank accounts will be frozen. Once the winding-up process begins, the director may not use the company's assets other than to swell them for the benefit of creditors whose interests are now paramount.

Throughout the insolvency process, you should be working to preserve and increase the value of the company's assets so they can be realised and the proceeds distributed to creditors. Strictly speaking, under these circumstances all payments and any use of the company's assets should be validated by the court.

Validation Orders

To obtain a validation order, you must send information to the court about any payment(s) you intend to make. This should be accompanied by a witness statement explaining how creditors will benefit if the court authorises the payment. The validation order may be granted if the debt is disputed and you can prove the company is stable, profitable and solvent. However, the application is likely to fail if the company is insolvent.

It helps if you can demonstrate the petition is mischievous. In these circumstances, the court wants to hear:

- The debt is disputed
- There is no money owed
- The petition will eventually be dismissed when the case is heard properly

Post-Petition Transactions

Directors are personally liable for all transactions and payments made from the company's bank account(s) after a winding up order if they did not first obtain a validation order.

When a liquidator investigates a company that has been placed into compulsory liquidation, one of the first things they look for is post-petition transactions in contrary of section 127 of the Insolvency Act 1986. Consequently, if a liquidator discovers transactions left the company bank account after the petition was issued, they will say to the director(s):

'You allowed these payments to be made, which effectively reduced the company's assets during the course of its winding up. As a result, you're personally liable for those losses.'

Still, a debtor who is going to pay the debt and have the winding-up petition withdrawn or dismissed may make as many post-petition transactions as they like. The danger comes if another creditor tries to bring a petition and fails because there is already a petition in place. The second creditor will probably join the first petition and may encourage others to join. If this happens, the director will have to pay off multiple creditors, which could become a huge financial burden.

In such circumstances, the director(s) cannot allow the company to be wound up because they will be liable for all the post-petition transactions. The only way out of this conundrum is to place the business into a statutory insolvency procedure such as a:

- Creditors' voluntary liquidation (CVL), which will make all post-petition transactions invalid, or a
- Company voluntary arrangement (CVA), which allows insolvent companies

to continue trading while repaying creditors over three to five years.

Defending a Petition

Creditors often use winding-up petitions to force debtors/company directors to pay overdue debts because they know once a petition has been served the debtor company's assets will be paralyzed and you will be forced to:

- Pay the debt
- Seek a court injunction
- Go to court for a validation order

A director whose company is unable to pay its debts should never be surprised to receive a winding-up petition, especially as in most cases they would have received a statutory demand requesting payment in 21 days. There are several ways to quickly defeat a winding-up petition, but two are particularly ingenious.

First, a debtor/director whose company may be insolvent can overcome a winding-up petition by applying for a court injunction. The serving of a windingup petition for a disputed debt is an abuse of the court process. As a result, the petition will be deemed invalid if you can demonstrate how the debt is disputed and you would not have to prove the company's solvency.

You are more likely to be successful if the company is solvent, and if the injunction is granted the petitioner is likely to pay all costs, which could be between £10,000 and £15,000, or more if the injunction is resisted.

Alternatively, you (the debtor/director) can dispute the debt and make an application to the court for a validation order. This should work perfectly for a solvent company because if the order is granted, the winding-up petition is likely to be dismissed when the case is heard, and the petitioner will probably have to pay all costs, which could range from £5,000 to £20,000 in advance.

Disputed Debts

It is always best to raise any disputes before a winding-up petition has been issued. However, if you can show evidence of a genuine dispute, the petition must be withdrawn immediately. Responding to a winding-up petition by creating a dispute in the county court gives a debtor who either cannot or will not pay an additional six months to negotiate a settlement while the petitioner incurs further legal expenses.

Similarly, if the winding-up petition has been issued without a court judgment you can argue the petition is being used as a debt collection tool, which is an abuse of the court process. It is entirely down to the court's discretion whether the court will support or reject your claim. Some courts will be sympathetic to a petitioner chasing an old invoice, but others will say:

'This is not a debt collection court. You should've got a county court judgment before commencing with winding-up proceedings.'

Alternative Dispute Resolutions

You should always ensure alternative dispute resolutions are included in the purchase orders when establishing a relationship with a new supplier. A savvy debtor will have the following written somewhere on their purchase orders:

'All disputes of any nature, including unpaid invoices, shall be referred to either arbitration or mediation.'

This essential addition stops creditors from litigating unpaid invoices. It also keeps costs down by ensuring that any disputes will be resolved outside of the county court. Furthermore, there are no wider ramifications because whatever you agree with the creditor can be legally binding.

When buying goods and services, a progressive debtor will give the creditor the purchase order, and say:

'I'm buying your goods subject to the terms of my purchase order. When you send your invoice, please quote the purchase order reference number to make it easier for both of us to track the payment.'

Once a creditor adds the purchase order reference number onto their invoice, they will be deemed to have accepted the debtor's terms of the purchase.

COMPULSORY LIQUIDATION

The process of a compulsory liquidation usually starts when an unpaid creditor files a winding-up petition in court against a company they believe is insolvent. If the court agrees to make the order, the case is sent to the official receiver, a court official employed by the government's Insolvency Service.

OFFICIAL RECEIVER INTERVIEWS

When a company becomes the subject of a compulsory winding-up order, the court draws up an order and makes a ruling effectively to end the company's existence. The order is sent to the government's Insolvency Service where it is administered and forwarded to a civil servant officer of the court, the Official Receiver. The office of the Official Receiver deals with all new bankruptcy and company winding-up orders for the court.

If there are no assets to be realised, but there is money in the company's bank account(s), the Official Receiver may act as an interim liquidator and ask for the cash to be transferred into the company's liquidation estate. They will use the information you provide to produce a statement of affairs, which is shared with creditors to explain why the company has been wound up.

However, the Official Receiver will randomly select a local insolvency practitioner to liquidate the company on behalf of the Secretary of State for Business, Energy and Industrial Strategy if the company has physical assets and there are investigations to be conducted.

Official Receiver Examination

As part of the winding-up process, an examiner from the Official Receiver's office may summon anyone who had a relationship with the company in the three years leading up to its demise. Usually, the company director is summoned to the

Insolvency Service to be interviewed about their business affairs and conduct. However, in order to gain a comprehensive understanding of the insolvency the Official Receiver may request interviews with as many people connected to the company as necessary.

Before the interview, you will be asked to complete a questionnaire detailing the company's:

- Assets
- Liabilities
- Creditors
- Staff
- Financial affairs
- Business activities

You should either bring the completed questionnaire to the interview or post it back to the Official Receiver beforehand.

How Should a Director Prepare?

The best approach for the Official Receiver's examination is to be open and honest, and to explain all the steps taken to protect the interests of the company's creditors, shareholders and employees and Her Majesty's Revenue & Customs (HMRC).

The interview can take anything between one and three hours, depending on:

- What you say
- The information you've provided in the questionnaire
- The complexity of the insolvency

There will probably be some acute issues you are either unaware of or have forgotten about that will need to be attended to by a professional prior to the interview.

The Official Receiver and examiner act solely in the interest of the company's creditors, so are unable to provide you with advice that is in your best interest. You may therefore wish to seek an independent professional for counsel around the issues that require attention to limit any adverse consequences against you, such as personal liability claims, director disqualification proceedings or worse.

Allegations of Misconduct

The examiner looks for evidence of misconduct (also known as misfeasance) by the director(s) and will try to determine whether the trust creditors put in the company and its director(s) was misplaced or abused. Although the Official Receiver will investigate the monies owed to creditors and the revenue collected by the company on behalf of HMRC, it is important to understand their primary concern is the directors' behaviour, not the amount of money creditors lost.

Examiners ask lots of questions and seek to identify areas where the director(s) may have committed acts of misfeasance. But if they believe mistakes were entrepreneurial rather than malicious, the director(s) will not be severely reprimanded.

For example, a director who acted with integrity but lost creditors £10 million will probably not be severely punished. However, a dishonest and irresponsible director who squandered £100,000 of customers' deposits is likely to face disqualification proceedings.

A director found to have committed a serious misfeasance could also be forced to:

- Return any property (including money) taken from the company prior to its demise

- Make a significant financial contribution into the liquidation estate

Preferential Payments

In the months leading up to and during insolvency, the company would have collected taxes from VAT, National Insurance and PAYE. But was any of this money handed over to HMRC, and if not what happened to the exchequer's revenue?

In many instances, a competent insolvency practitioner will be able to highlight how money that should have been sent to HMRC was used to repay the director's loan account or compensate friends and suppliers the director was planning to bring over to a new business. Either way, both examples would reveal evidence of preferential treatment to creditors at the expense of HMRC.

If there are assets to be realised, the liquidator will do a lot of searching and conduct intrusive investigations to find out:

- Who was paid
- When they were paid
- If there are patterns of behaviour that demonstrate preferential treatment between the director and any of the creditors

Directors' Conduct D-Report

Depending on the type of liquidation, either the liquidator or Official Receiver will file to the Insolvency Service a Directors' Conduct D-Report, which is a confidential document outlining the director's behaviour.

To prevent liquidators and Official Receivers straying from the truth, the D-Report is quite prescriptive and asks questions such as:

- How many creditors are involved and when were they last paid?
- How much is owed to HMRC and when was the last tax payment made?

- When were orders placed?
- What are the dates of the last invoices?
- How many purchases were made in the months leading up to insolvency?

Just like the Official Receiver examination, the whole idea of the D-Report is to identify bad behaviour and misfeasance.

For example, from the D-Report it would be easy to establish that a company with an average monthly spend of £50,000 began purchasing £100,000 worth of goods in the six months prior to insolvency. If revenues were falling, such a huge jump in monthly spending is suspicious and suggests the director(s) knew the company was collapsing but chose to expose creditors to greater risk by taking on more stock.

If the director(s) was to respond by saying they took on more stock to sell items cheaper and bring in more revenue for creditors, it would be relatively easy to confirm or refute their claim by making further investigations into:

- How the stock was sold
- Where it went
- Who it was sold to
- How much the stock was sold for
- The amounts sold
- Sale dates

The D-Report is submitted to the Secretary of State for Business, Energy and Industrial Strategy. Director disqualification proceedings may follow if its content raises any serious questions about the director's conduct, especially if they owe significant debts to HMRC.

Lost Accounts, Books and Records

It is surprising how many directors turn up for interviews claiming to have 'lost' the company's accounts, books and records. This is pretty senseless because although the missing books may prevent the Official Receiver and liquidator from conducting a thorough examination, they will simply formulate their own books by requesting copies of invoices, statements and receipts from creditors and the bank.

Losing the company's physical books and records is almost impossible because even if a director has misplaced their server and hard drive the vast majority of the information held on their laptop is stored via cloud computing and can never be permanently erased.

Moreover, the Official Receiver is likely to recommend disqualification proceedings if you attend the examination without the company's books and records because according to section 386 of the Companies Act 2006, a director must maintain company accounting records for up to six years, and failure to deliver them upon request is an offence.

Creditors' Voluntary Liquidation

In a creditors' voluntary liquidation (CVL), the liquidator examines the director(s) as the Official Receiver would, but the examination is less formal. For example, interviews are sometimes conducted via telephone. Similarly, some directors of insolvent companies opt for a CVL because they will get to nominate the liquidator, whereas the liquidator is appointed by the Official Receiver in a compulsory liquidation.

Consequently, liquidators investigating compulsory liquidations target directors far more aggressively and will turn their lives upside down in an effort to generate more revenue for themselves and creditors.

Dealing with Liquidators

The role of the liquidator is sometimes contradictory because although they are supposed to protect creditors' interests in compulsory liquidations, complaints of excessive liquidator fees are common. Equally conflicting is the notion that a liquidator in a CVL is supposed to protect creditors' interests because they must first cosy up to the company's director(s) to get the job.

The sad truth is few directors will appoint a shrewd and tenacious liquidator with a solid reputation for putting creditors' interests first. As a result, a liquidator must learn to compromise if they want regular employment. Conversely, there are some questionable liquidators who take advantage of gullible directors to enrich themselves at the expense of creditors.

For example, a greedy liquidator in a creditors' voluntary liquidation may tell the director(s) who appointed them:

'I need to make some money from this job. Before you go into liquidation, can you leave behind some assets that I can sell or a few debtors with unpaid invoices that I can chase up?'

Initially, the liquidator may become friendly with the director(s). But if there are insufficient or no assets to recover, they will transfer their allegiance. Instead of working in partnership, the liquidator will start investigating the director(s) and coerce them into putting money into the liquidation estate, under the pretence that creditors are demanding more money.

Similarly, if the liquidator believes a director is trying to evade or outsmart them, they may try to extract greater fees and threaten to file an uncomplimentary

D-Report. For example, a questionable liquidator who is trying to frighten an unsuspecting director may say something like:

'The creditors have formed a committee and claim to have evidence of some wrongdoing by you and your colleagues, which they want me to investigate. They want me to criticise you in the D-Report, but if you put some more money into the liquidation estate I think they'll cool off.'

DIRECTOR DISQUALIFICATION PROCEEDINGS

What are Disqualification Proceedings?

If you are a registered, shadow or de facto director accused of misfeasance while managing a company, you could find yourself subject to director disqualification proceedings in accordance with the Company Directors Disqualification Act 1986.

Director disqualification proceedings will commence and be based upon a claim that as the director of a company now in insolvency you committed a serious act of misconduct and are therefore unfit to direct or manage the affairs of another company.

Consequences

Without a court's permission, a disqualified director cannot be involved in any aspect of a company or limited liability partnership, including its:

- Formation
- Marketing
- Management

Additionally, you will be personally liable for the losses of any business you are involved in while disqualified and could face criminal prosecution.

Length of Bans

Depending on the severity of the misconduct, you could be banned from being a company director for anything between two and 15 years, which may detrimentally affect your long-term career.

In recent years, the government agency responsible for investigating wrongdoing by directors, the Insolvency Service, has targeted serious and serial offenders with tougher sentences. According to the agency's figures, the average monthly number of directors disqualified for five to 15 years rose steadily between 2010 and 2016 to 48.

The increase is evidence of a clampdown on directors who:

- Trade while insolvent
- Transfer assets into a new business to avoid paying creditors
- Make preferential payments to friends, family and other connected creditors

As a result, the terms of most disqualifications now range from five to 10 years. This includes offences such as:

- Fraud
- 'Losing' the company's accounts
- Failure to return deposits paid by online customers

Director Disqualification Undertakings

A director who admits misfeasance can disqualify themselves voluntarily with a director disqualification undertaking (DDU), so there is no need for court proceedings. The courts and Insolvency Service want to avoid unnecessary spending and will consider reducing the length of a ban in exchange for a DDU.

Moreover, the costs for an investigation cannot be recovered from a director whose DDU was accepted before the commencement of court proceedings.

Subsequently, to avoid any potential court costs, many directors facing disqualification proceedings offer an undertaking at the earliest opportunity.

DEFENDING A MISFEASANCE ACTION

What is Misfeasance?

In accordance with section 212 of the Insolvency Act 1986, misfeasance takes place when a director or ex-director has misapplied, misappropriated, retained or become accountable for any of the company's money or property.

Misfeasance is far worse than maladministration because it means a director has been dishonest and engaged in bad behaviour, wrongdoing or some misconduct that's brought financial loss to creditors.

Who Can Bring a Misfeasance Claim?

In the vast majority of cases, the insolvency practitioner (liquidator) will claim for misfeasance against the director of a liquidated company. The government's Insolvency Service, creditors and shareholders can also take action. However, no claim can be made if the business has entered a company voluntary arrangement (CVA).

Examples of Misfeasance

A director who removes assets from a company or sells them to a friend at an undervalued price is committing a misfeasance.

Other examples include:

- Making preferential payments to creditors

- Failing to repay a director's loan account
- Avoidance of property dispositions
- Misconduct during the course of winding-up proceedings

In the most serious situations investigators may scrutinise a director's conduct for the three years prior to the insolvency, especially if the misfeasance caused or accelerated the company's demise.

Probably the worst acts of misfeasance are:

1) Fraud, which can result in a director being sent to prison.
2) False accounting whereby a director deliberately misrepresents a company's balance sheet to encourage lenders and suppliers to offer credit.

Tips and Advice

Above all, never cave in to threats of misfeasance proceedings in written correspondence from a liquidator, creditor, shareholder or their lawyers. Only take these warnings seriously after court documents have been served because that is when things can get costly.

There is very little a liquidator, creditors or shareholders can do if you decide to be stubborn and unyielding. Unless:

- The case involves fraud, or
- The court can be persuaded that you are a spendthrift who will either dissipate all of the assets and money or move them beyond the court's jurisdiction.

Misfeasance claims can be stressful and cost between £30,000 and £60,000, or even more, to defend.

Preferential Payments

A competent insolvency practitioner/liquidator will chronicle the company's bank statements and try to identify a pattern of preferential payments to connected suppliers and lenders the director is friendly with. Similarly, although the company would have collected National Insurance, VAT and PAYE tax revenue in the months prior to insolvency, HM Revenue & Customs probably never received any of that money. As a result, any other creditor that received payments from the company during the same period would be deemed to have received preferential treatment, which is a misfeasance.

If the investigation is conducted by the Insolvency Service, their representatives may commence director disqualification proceedings on the grounds that you discriminated against HMRC by withholding their funds and using the money to pay other creditors.

If a liquidator has evidence that you continued to trade despite long periods of insolvency, which caused creditors to suffer loss, they will try to make you pay money into the liquidation estate.

Deals Between the Director(s) and Liquidator

If a company director owes £200,000 but decides to only acknowledge £50,000 of the debt, the insolvency practitioner/liquidator can:

- Accept the payment
- Negotiate for more money
- Go to court

An insolvency practitioner who decides to litigate will have access to plenty of law firms, but limited resources to fund the action. Nevertheless, they work closely with lawyers so it is easy for them to get one to send the director(s) a letter before action. Additionally, the liquidator may seek the assistance of a litigation funder who will fund the case in exchange for around 50% of the proceeds.

But this only happens if you are in funds and there is clear evidence of misfeasance because liquidators are fearful of launching court proceedings without a litigation funder, losing and then having to explain why creditors' money was used to finance an unsuccessful action.

When a liquidator sends a letter before action and starts probing for money, some directors capitulate quickly and cut a deal, while others need more convincing. Still, at some stage everyone involved has to negotiate a deal. For example, a director who owes creditors £400,000, but is only taking responsibility for £50,000 might say to the liquidator:

'I've got £40,000 plus £10,000 for your costs: take it or leave it. If you pursue the court action, you should consider that I'm involved in litigations with other parties. As a result, my situation can easily change and I may have no money or assets by the time your proceedings have finished.'

Third-Party Payments

The creditor who launched the action may approach you to negotiate a thirdparty payment. If you agree, it is important to remember any disbursement that comes directly from the proceeds of the insolvent company is a preferential payment.

However, it's perfectly legal for a person unconnected to the action and company to make a one-off disbursement (paid either as a single sum or in instalments), as this would simply be a third-party payment to reimburse the creditor in recognition of their loss. In these circumstances, both parties would sign a non-disclosure agreement to keep the details of the deal confidential.

To avoid obstructions from the liquidator, the creditor should immediately apply to the court to either:

- Discontinue the misfeasance action, or
- Obtain a consent order to confirm that both parties have agreed to discontinue the proceedings.

MORATORIUM

A moratorium is a statutory insolvency procedure that shields a company from its creditors for a minimum of 20 business days.

During this period, pre-moratorium debts do not have to be paid and the company receives considerable protection from:

- Landlords
- Legal actions
- Insolvency proceedings

Current liabilities such as rent, loans and wages must be paid for during the moratorium and the company will be prohibited from:

- Granting securities
- Obtaining credit of more than £500

The company's directors must appoint an insolvency practitioner/monitor to oversee day-to-day operations. This should provide director(s) with enough time to:

- Remodel the business
- Secure additional investment

There are two ways a director can place a company into a moratorium:

1) The in-court process, which involves making an application to the court. The moratorium commences as soon as a court order is made.

2) The out-of-court process, which starts when the relevant documents have been filed at court. This process is similar to appointing an administrator. But, unlike the administration procedure, directors don't have to notify floating charge holders beforehand.

The necessary documents that must be filed at the court for either process are identical and include statements from the:

- Director(s) confirming the company either cannot or will soon be unable to pay its debts
- Monitor(s) confirming that a moratorium would help to rescue the company

If a winding-up petition has been issued against the company, a moratorium order will only be granted if the court decides this is the best option for creditors.

In these circumstances, the court may also make an order for the company to be:

- Wound up, or
- Placed into administration or another statutory insolvency procedure

If necessary, the company director(s) may seek to extend the duration of the moratorium for:

- Another 20 business days without consent, or
- Longer than 20 days with the consent of either the court or pre-moratorium creditors

A monitor may terminate the moratorium prematurely if they decide the company can no longer be rescued. Furthermore, monitors must inform Companies House and all creditors that a moratorium is in place. As a result, it is likely that suppliers will stop offering goods and services on credit.

Although creditors may not commence another statutory insolvency procedure during the moratorium, an astute director will use the time granted by the moratorium period to prepare a proposal that will place their company into either:

1) Administration, or
2) A company voluntary arrangement (CVA)

Both procedures offer excellent restructuring opportunities, depending on the director's objective. Alternatively, director(s) can use a creditors' voluntary liquidation (CVL) to wind up a failing company.

Insolvency issues can be complex. Although lawyers are useful, ultimately they will refer you to an insolvency practitioner who has a duty to protect the company's creditors, which sometimes creates a conflict of interest for directors.

To avoid this happening, shrewd directors seek support from independent professionals who will:

- Develop a strategy to restructure the business
- Provide impartial advice on statutory and alternative procedures
- Work alongside the insolvency practitioner
- Ensure the insolvency practitioner charges reasonable fees

EPILOGUE

Irrespective of your profession or job title, personal and corporate insolvency play such a huge role in modern life that they are virtually impossible to avoid. As a result, this book is dedicated to helping the perplexed debtors I speak with daily who want to protect themselves and learn how to affect and control the course of insolvency proceedings.

As the director of multi-award-winning consultancy firm Insolvency & Law, I have spent more than 12 years providing countless numbers of debtors with support, guidance and advice. Accordingly, the chapters you have just completed are my earnest attempt to coalesce all of this knowledge and experience into an easy-to-read, palatable and jargon-free book that simplifies business rescue, debt recovery and insolvency procedures.

My primary objective is to encourage insolvents entering insolvency procedures to stop viewing themselves as lambs to the slaughter, wholly at the mercy of the insolvency practitioners they hire.

The average person is unfamiliar with the United Kingdom's insolvency laws because in most cases business owners will engage the services of a lawyer or an accountant continuously. But they only find use for an insolvency practitioner when something goes wrong.

I first came into contact with this industry in 1993 when I had a business that I was considering placing into insolvency. I contacted an insolvency practitioner who, in his attempt to secure the job, explained that if I wanted I could easily buy the assets back from the business.

'There won't be anything left for creditors... but who cares about them anyway? If they're careless enough to supply goods on credit without doing due diligence, they only have themselves to blame,' he said.

In the end, I decided against insolvency, carried on trading and eventually sold the business. But the insolvency practitioner's words made me consider for the first time the importance of protecting my assets.

I was enlightened further in 1994 when I began working for a corporate debt recovery company. There, I gained first-hand knowledge of how insolvent companies would go bust, immediately set up another business using the same staff and premises and carry on trading having lost all of the liabilities. And all of this was done with the aid of insolvency practitioners, which led me to understand the conflicting nature of their work.

Brief History of Insolvency Legislation

In the early 1980s, Prime Minister Margaret Thatcher announced plans to boost Britain's economy by deregulating the financial markets and transforming the City of London into a central hub for global finance. But the scheme was initially hampered by a series of huge corporate failings, including the collapse of Laker Airways in 1982 and Johnson Matthey Bankers two years later.

Another stumbling block was the illegal share-trading conspiracy known as the Guinness Scandal, which involved an employee at HM Queen Elizabeth II's favourite stockbroking firm, Cazenove, and former Guinness chairman Ernest Saunders who was jailed for conspiracy, false accounting and theft, along with millionaire trader Anthony Parnes and the CEO of property developers Heron

International, Gerald Ronson.

The Guinness Scandal was the biggest mainstream media story during the summer of 1986 and possibly encouraged the government to hurry through new legislation that would simultaneously restructure the economy as well as silence critics who questioned their ability to regulate the financial system.

Subsequently, on 25 July 1986, Thatcher's government enacted the UK's first piece of insolvency legislation, the Insolvency Act 1986, and began deregulating the financial markets with a landmark event known as the 'Big Bang' three months later.

The new laws drew mostly from the recommendations of a 1984 White Paper, A Revised Framework for Insolvency Law, written by accountant Kenneth Cork who the Labour government commissioned in 1977 to investigate the modernisation of insolvency procedures. Cork, who acquired monikers such as 'the insolvency baron' and 'the great liquidator', was later knighted for his pioneering work, which introduced the administration procedure and a general rescue culture into British business. It took almost 15 years and a change of government before any amendments would be made to Cork's recommendations.

In the early 2000s, Prime Minister Tony Blair and Chancellor of the Exchequer Gordon Brown launched a series of initiatives aimed at establishing their 'New Labour' project as a pro-business government. Some of these ideas were in response to calls by business groups to soften the insolvency rules and resulted in the passing of the Enterprise Act 2002, which:

- Affected several insolvency procedures
- Introduced pre-pack administrations
- Removed the status of HMRC as a preferential creditor (from 6 April 2020, HMRC regained its status as a preferred creditor in regards to VAT, income tax,

PAYE, employee NICs and Construction Industry Scheme deductions)

Blair and Brown understood that entrepreneurs are risk-takers who create employment and reduce the burden on the state when they are successful. They realised that rather than penalising business owners whose companies had collapsed, it was more productive to encourage entrepreneurs to dust themselves off, launch a new venture and quickly return to the marketplace.

As a result, the Enterprise Act 2002 made bankruptcy more popular and acceptable by:

- Reducing from three years to 12 months the time it takes for a bankrupt to be discharged.
- Lessening the time the procedure stays on a person's credit file from 11 years to six.

According to figures released by the government's Insolvency Service, personal insolvency procedures such as bankruptcies and individual voluntary arrangements jumped to a seven-year high in 2018, and the number of corporate insolvencies recorded during the first three months of the year rose by 6% in 2019.

It is estimated the UK's 1,735 insolvency practitioners earn more than £1bn in fees annually, so insolvency is clearly a thriving and prosperous business. But that is not the case for everyone, because in truth there are only three real earners and winners in insolvencies: insolvency practitioners, lawyers and valuation agents.

The purpose of this book and much of what I do on a daily basis is to redress the balance of power by driving down insolvency practitioner fees and helping insolvents to protect their assets. In the UK, insolvency practitioners are regulated by five trade associations, collectively known as Recognised Professional Bodies (RPBs):

- Insolvency Practitioners Association
- Institute of Chartered Accountants in England and Wales
- Association of Chartered Certified Accountants
- Institute of Chartered Accountants of Scotland
- Chartered Accountants Ireland

It is unclear exactly what these organisations do as all complaints against insolvency practitioners are dealt with by the Insolvency Service and most are rejected. On average, RPBs received more than 15 complaints every week in 2017, a total of 757 throughout the year. Yet it is hard to find any substantive data on an insolvency practitioner's performance or how they are punished for transgressions, as RPBs are exempt from Freedom of Information requests. But we do know that no insolvency practitioners were banned in 2017 and very few sanctions were issued.

Considering the huge and vital role insolvency practitioners play in the corporate world, they operate with an extraordinary lack of transparency, 50 which makes it almost impossible to evaluate their performance individually or collectively. Consequently, there's no way for an insolvent to research and verify whether an insolvency practitioner has a good reputation.

Through Insolvency & Law and this book, I am attempting to challenge some of the glaring inconsistencies that are to be found in the insolvency regime and will continue delivering customer-focused representation and advocacy services because whether you are an individual struggling to avoid financial ruin or a company director trying to protect yourself from adverse proceedings, everyone deserves to be treated fairly.